3

Garden Ornaments and Antiques

Myra Yellin Outwater
Photography by Eric B. Outwater

4880 Lower Valley Road, Atglen, PA 19310 USA

Dedication

To my mother who taught me that every garden, no matter how small, is a constant source of joy.

Designed by "Sue"
Typeset in ZapfChan Bd BT/Dutch801 Rm BT

ISBN: 0-7643-1125-5
Printed in China
1 2 3 4

Library of Congress Cataloging-in-Publication Data

Outwater, Myra Yellin.
    Garden ornaments & antiques/Myra Yellin Outwater.
        p. cm.
    ISBN 0-7643-1125-5 (hardcover)
    1. Garden ornaments and furniture. I. Title.
SB473.5.O88 2000
717-dc21   00-008502

Published by Schiffer Publishing Ltd.
4880 Lower Valley Road
Atglen, PA 19310
Phone: (610) 593-1777; Fax: (610) 593-2002
E-mail: Schifferbk@aol.com
Please visit our web site catalog at
www.schifferbooks.com

We are always looking for people to write books on new and related subjects. If you have an idea for a book, please contact us at the above address.

This book may be purchased from the publisher.
Include $3.95 for shipping.
Please try your bookstore first.
You may write for a free catalog.

In Europe, Schiffer books are distributed by:
Bushwood Books
6 Marksbury Ave.
Kew Gardens
Surrey TW9 4JF England
Phone: 44 (0)208 392-8585; Fax: 44 (0)208 392-9876
E-mail: Bushwd@aol.com
Free postage in the UK. Europe: air mail at cost.

Monika Dornan.

Contents

Monika Dorman.

Acknowledgments

Urs Oeggerli
Lynette G. Proler
Keith Nix
Jennifer B. Shattuck
Moshe Bronstein
Larry Keller
Joe Fizzano
Ron Heffelfinger
Karen Babcock
Sam Kenworthy
Richard Schultz
Judy and Michael Kraynick
Larry Beck
and Paul Mackerer,
who designed the gardens at the Pondhouse.

All these people have shared their knowledge, invited us into their gardens, and been wonderful guides to the beauty of garden art. Also, to Monika Dorman, for her fabulous contributions of flower photography, and Jennifer Lindbeck, for her valued time and editiorial support.

Monika Dorman.

Introduction
Garden Meditations

It always surprises me that when I mention winter to my gardening friends, their gaze becomes dull, and their conversation pedantic. They talk about catalogs and plans but never plantings.

For us, our winter gardens are as much gardens of discovery as those of the spring and summer. We like to survey our garden in the late fall and in the snow and check for unexpected glimpses of nature's wonder. The discovery of an old bird's nest is suddenly revealed, bare on a leafless branch. Grasses, now aged sentries, are bowed and bent from snow. Ponds, partially frozen, become glacial moonscapes of white and silver tufted grasses swaying in the wind. Dead, shriveled flowers become tiny mushroom caps and gnome-like figures.

It's the crocuses that first signal the arrival of spring in our garden. Their tiny, fragile, white and purple blossoms seem so delicate, as if they would tremble in terror against the still angry blustering gusts of March winds. And yet, each spring, it is their stalwart and graceful show of defiance that stirs my gardening juices.

The arrival of snowdrops, and then crocuses always comes so suddenly and unexpectedly. One day the garden is dead, filled with decay and debris, and the next day, it is filled with the promise of beauty. Whenever I see these small tightly folded blossoms poking out of the snow and the straggly leaf-strewn, dried rutted earth, I am filled with a new sense of energy and vigor. Gone is my winter torpor. Away with work. On with a sweater and gloves, and off I go, racing outside to inspect my beds. That one tentative burst of pale color has alerted me that spring is almost here, summer is approaching, and it's time to complete gardening plans.

In the winter, we read books, study catalogs, and dream visions on a grand scale. We fancy competing with long-gone gardeners of fabled estates and villas in Europe, back to the days when the landed gentry, oblivious to the mundane laborious nature of gardening, ordered labyrinths, mazes, follies, topiaries, and manicured boxwood hedges to grace their homes.

In our winter dreams, money is no object, our energy is unlimited, and the realities of rock, shade, and poor soil lie hidden in the dim recesses of our imaginations. But once the spring sun warms the soil, and the prospect of marathon days spent planting, digging, and weeding is imminent, our determination to create masses of color becomes overwhelming.

Each year, our gardening dreams are larger than our energies and our budgets. We head to nurseries to satisfy overly ambitious winter plans. And then sobered by reality, we shop like frugal puritans, halving our expectations.

For the first few weeks of spring, I am like Sherlock Holmes with a mental magnifying glass, checking for signs of the mounds of daffodil bulbs planted in a fall frenzy, and patrolling beds against the ravages of hungry squirrels and chipmunks. I stay up late at night worrying if the gaudy extravagance of my tulip-spending spree will bloom into brilliant splashes of color. I return my terra cotta figures to their rightful posts in the garden, and check the stone cherub for signs of winter cracks. (Somehow she always survives, ready to once more wear her summer dress of ivy chains and rose blossoms.)

All winter I anchor my dreams to the whims of nature. I dream hopefully about lush plantings, cross my fingers that we will be spared drought or too much rain, or an attack from ravenous rabbits or insects like Japanese beatles.

But then the spring unfolds and I realize that all is out of my control. The daffodils bloom. The tulips fall to the ground, a mound of color. The peonies explode. Honesty blossoms. And the stately June iris stand tall. By the time the saucy daisies and the flounces of day lilies appear, our ponds are complete. Then the roses bloom, and we plant the work force of color—impatiens, zinnias, and my gypsies—cleome and cosmos. It's a wonder to me that these small seeds reseed and reseed, popping up everywhere, respecting no barriers, neither cracks in my walks nor spaces in the gravel and stones.

The best part is the early morning inspection, the afternoon contemplation, and the excitement brought each day by new surprises and new successes. Some days I sit watching the sunlight dance on my pond, forming syncopated reflections as the shadows flicker back and forth on the surface and a ballet duo of shimmering dragonflies twirl about.

Gardens like people are never perfect, rarely predictable, never finished, and always promise more.

Upscaling a Garden

My mother always looked forward to a blue garden in June. Iris were among her favorite flowers. They are still my favorites, too. *Photo courtesy of Jerry Caliendo.*

I grew up with small scale gardens. Our first home in Connecticut was a two-family row house, with a pocket-sized backyard and slivers of grass lining a driveway we shared with our neighbors. Our first garden was built on flashy displays of annuals. My mother planted zinnias, salvia, marigolds, and sweet William. She hesitantly planted a few tulips, daffodils, and iris.

When I was a teenager, we bought another house, a Norman-Tudor house, with terraced flower beds, established roses, rhododendrons, azaleas, mountain laurel, and a side porch that reminded my mother of the shade gardens of the tropics. We moved in, in the fall. By early spring, my mother had designs for a blue June garden, full of pansies, Johnny jump-ups, tulips, iris, phlox, delphinium, and cornflowers. Next she planted hundreds of pachysandra down our front hill and then sat back and planned the way that she would stamp her personality on the remaining two terraces.

My favorite spot was the porch, furnished with bamboo garden furniture, that would later remind me of Noel Coward and friends lounging at Raffles Hotel in Singapore. My mother planted hostas, lilies of the valley, and other luxurious plantings—I no longer remember their names. When she was done, she bought a pair of shiny, deep ocean blue majolica urns and placed them at the entrance to her shade garden. I still have one. I fill it with geraniums to remind me of her.

Our garden had a hut at the top of the hill with a flagstone patio, a wooden picnic table, and two graceful, albeit lopsided, wicker side chairs. I adopted one of the chairs as my own, and would move it around the garden and dream of the days when I would be a famous writer and someone would publish my poetry.

For years after my parents sold the house, my mother maintained a proprietary interest in her garden. Each year she would buy a ticket to see her house when it was offered on house tours. I still remember the trauma of the year that the house was sold to non-gardeners, Philistines, who tore out the flowers and flattened the terraces to create a larger lawn. My mother was in tears. Until then I think she still envisioned the house as hers, driving by it each spring to inspect her gardens and watch her flowers and bushes grow.

Until the day she died, my mother tried to micromanage my garden from afar. "Plant salvia. Plant iris. Plant pachysandra and roses and sweet William. Plant marigolds in the summer, they keep away rabbits, and don't forget chrysanthemums in the fall."

Each spring I would follow my own desires. I never liked salvia, marigolds, nor chrysanthemums.

A week after my mother died, a friend invited my husband and me to dinner. His garden had been newly landscaped. There were circular beds of salvia, marigolds, and sweet William. I felt good. Mother was there in spirit.

20th century blue majolica urn with pedestal. $500-800.

The Function of a Garden Antique and Ornament

When most people think of garden decor, they immediately think of elegant, delicate, lush flower beds and exotic plantings. Few think of a garden as an outdoor gallery space for weather-resistant art. And yet, if a garden is an outdoor living space, then shouldn't it be like a well-designed interior room, filled with art and ornament?

Garden ornaments and antiques fulfill the same function as indoor art and sculpture. They create design focal points. They beautify spaces and provide visual pleasure. Imagine a lawn of endless green grass. Then close your eyes and envision an arbor of manicured boxwoods. Insert a simple marble birdbath or a three-tiered fountain, a graceful female nude perhaps, or a ferocious pair of lions. Possibly surround the garden with an ornate cast iron fence. Imagine a garden bench, or set out an elegant marble table. Create a stone patio. Add two wooden rocking chairs or an aluminum lounge chair.

Can you see the difference?

Imagine the joy you'll feel when you see the first perfectly formed tulip or rose of the season. Revel in the first blooms of lilacs and forsythia. Find repose in an arbor or an alcove. Gain a sense of antiquity from a grouping of elegant marble goddesses, or a pair of nineteenth-century lead garden figures, the male holding his spade poised, the woman holding a bouquet of flowers.

That's what this book is about.

Gardens have inspired artists for centuries. One of the most famous is Monet's garden at Giverny, France. *Photo courtesy of Jerry Caliendo.*

Flowers can be planted in carefully designed beds such as this formal garden in Germany.

Others believe that structured plantings and manicured, patterned grasses enhance a home. Lanark Manor, Lanark, Pennsylvania.

18th century English garden designers such as Capability Brown believed in romanticized, natural-looking gardens and introduced bridges, natural paths, and walkways. This Westchester, New York garden has a romanticized pond. *The Garden Antiquary.*

Topiary trees have enhanced gardens for centuries. *Ladew Topiary Gardens, Monkton, Maryland.*

Cypress moss and yellow daisies are common in southern gardens.
Magnolia Gardens, Charleston, South Carolina.

The swamp at the Audubon Gardens, Magnolia Gardens, Charleston, South Carolina.

Imagine this scene without the columns, the statuary, the fountain, and the pool. Old Westbury Gardens, Old Westbury, New York.

Autumn. The Pondhouse.

Modern sculptures such as *Pocket Knife* by Pennsylvania sculptor Dan Kainz create an intimate outdoor space. Spring. The Pondhouse, Center Valley, Pennsylvania.

Right and above:
Trees, Kadishman, 60 tons, bronze, 1987. Israeli sculptor Kadishman created these metal sculptures of positive and negative trees. *the Philip and Muriel Berman Collection.*

Discarded farm equipment can add interest to a garden. The Beck garden, Center Valley, Pennsylvania.

Villa Reale, in the village of Marlia, just a few miles outside of Lucca on Italy's east coast.

A garden alcove. Villa Reale, Italy.

Villa Torrigiani, Lucca, Italy.

An ornate mosaic gate at the entrance to the Villa d'Este Hotel on Lake Como, Italy.

Many formal gardens are inspired by classic Italian and French designs. This Texas garden is enhanced by its owner's careful choice of urns, statuary, columns, and arches. *Proler/Oeggerli.*

Villa d'Este, Lake Como, Italy.

At the end of the day, there is not a more pleasant way to enjoy a garden than in a comfortable, inviting seat. *Meadowbloom Gardens, Chester Spring, Pennsylvania.*

Trellises and espaliered trees. *Ladew Topiary Gardens.*

In the end, gardening is an act of love.

Gardens offer daily delights. The Beck Garden.

Garden Ornaments and Outdoor Garden Design

Europeans have always understood decor and style more than Americans. Italian villas, English estates, and French chateaux have had showplace gardens for hundreds of years. Europeans understood that gardens could be used as extensions of indoor entertaining. Yet, it wasn't until the nineteenth century that Americans began to think of gardens as more than functional sources of food, and later, in the twentieth century, that they developed their own sense of gardening lifestyles. It wasn't until after the Industrial Revolution that Americans shed their Puritan constraints, and theories about the garden moved slowly away from function to form.

European royalty built opulent additions to their palaces as a sign of their wealth and power. A private summer palace in Germany.

14

The earliest American horticultural societies date from the early 1800s. Thomas Jefferson, for example, was an avid gardener, involved with every detail of design for both his homes—Monticello and his weekend retreat, "Poplar Forest." Yet, when he wrote about his gardens, he did not refer to the extensive allees, vistas, fruit orchards, and vineyards that surrounded his property. Instead, he thought of his kitchen garden.

Jefferson is a prime example of the Renaissance American. Like many other members of the new American, monied class, he traveled often to Europe and sought to emulate a European lifestyle. Like his English and French contemporaries, he considered an impressive home surrounded by wonderful gardens a sign of status.

Classical Garden Ornaments in American Gardens

Today it seems as if almost every American garden, no matter its size or scale, has at least one piece of garden art—a birdbath, a fountain, a cherub, a birdhouse, a wishing well, or a pink flamingo. And yet there was a time when Americans thought of garden ornaments only in classical designs and placed marble statuary, columns, urns, and ornately carved fountains in their gardens.

Dovecotes have been in fashion since the 18th century when raising pigeons and doves were popular hobbies. A 20th century wooden dovecote. *Ladew Topiary Gardens*.

A classical Greek temple designed by Henry Ladew for his gardens in Monkton, Maryland. *Ladew Topiary Gardens*.

Nineteenth-century Americans looked to their European neighbors for taste; they bought their art in Europe and looked to the Europeans for ideas on garden design as well. However, with the advent of the Industrial Revolution, a new kind of American ingenuity and inventiveness was born. And by the mid-nineteenth century, American gardeners were inventing their own styles. Influenced as much by beauty as by function, the Americans stamped their own idiosyncratic personalities on their home gardens. European gardens had classical outbuildings such as temples, follies, and pergolas. American homes had outhouses, smokehouses, summer kitchens, and springhouses, which in deference to European classicism were often adorned with Greek-inspired columns, porticos, and covered walkways. As early as the 1800s, American gardeners, such as Jefferson, began modifing classical ideals to conform to the constraints of American weather. Today Jefferson's gardens at Monticello are a perfect example of a blend of classical dimensions and American pragmatism. And by the end of the nineteenth century, American capitalists were sending agents to Europe to buy European antiques and statuary for both the inside and outside of their homes.

Today American gardens, like the American lifestyle, are a blend of the old and new. It is not unusual to see American homes being built with a composite of architectural styles, nor is it uncommon for their gardens to be designed with the same idiosyncratic flair.

Americans have always struggled to free themselves from constraints—societal, historic, and stylistic. American society is one of flux and freedom and no where is this more apparent than in the garden. In our travels, we have seen gardens that rigidly adhere to traditional Pennsylvania German design, enclosed by white picket fences, that revolve around a center focus, with traditional plantings, guarded by an outlandish carved folk art animal or spirit. We have toured formal gardens in Texas suburbs with allees, boxed-in parterres, patios lined with glazed urns from Provence, all designed with meticulous attention to classical dimensions and scale, only to learn that many of these gardens were installed, almost in their entirety, months before. We have walked on meticulously laid stone paths, through ornate wrought iron gates, guarded by classical stone lions, to finally emerge into a

Ladew Topiary Gardens. Dovecotes have sold at auctions for $750-2,000.

hodge podge of eccentric hysteria—gardens filled with overwhelming, breathtaking color, flamboyant blooms, and a scatter-may-care profusion of plantings. We have visited classically restrained gardens in the South and also traveled to Italy to see the source of many of the ideas for formal garden design.

In Europe, one finds a reverential adherence to classic formality. Statuary, plantings, and furnishings reflect the same period or style. But Americans have had no hesitation taking the best from the past and stamping it with their own signature, and that's why it is not uncommon to find classical nude statues or mythological maidens in one part of an American garden and modernist lawn furniture on the patio. Or rustic English staddle stones near the entrance of a garden maintained by a staff of twelve, under the control of a master gardener inspired by the Orient.

What has been most interesting to us is to see the correlation between indoor decor and outdoor style. Through the past two centuries, we have noted that garden furnishings reflect both the architectural and the aesthetic styles of the day. Just as the furniture of the seventeenth and eighteenth centuries had classical motifs, so did garden design create gardens that looked back to classical Greece and Rome for models with alcoves filled with tributes to the gods of Greece and Rome. Walking through the grounds of Italian villas one finds a surfeit of mythological spirits, nymphs, satyrs, and women in flowing robes and tunics.

By the eighteenth and nineteenth centuries, furniture began to adopt architectural motifs—pediments, arches, lion and animal supports. Garden designers of the period ornamented their gardens with antiquities, ruins, and columns, and even reconstructed temples and pergolas.

Later as interior design evolved, one saw Chippendale, Queen Anne, Sheraton, and Chinoiserie influence outdoor furniture. In the nineteenth century, there was such a great fascination with the Orient that botanists such as Thomas Hooker were trekking to the Himalayas to bring back exotic specimens of rhododendrons, azaleas, and other exotic plantings. At the same time shipping agents were sending back Oriental export porcelain, china, and fabrics. Soon it was common to find the same influence of the Orient and Chinese fretwork found inside the homes, outside in the garden. Gardens filled with Chinese moon gates, buddhas, Chinese stone lanterns, Foo Dogs, and lattice type lawn chairs.

Towards the middle of the nineteenth century, the heavy Victorian influence was seen in ornate cast iron benches and chairs, baroque patterned lead urns and planters, and many tiered fountains.

By the beginning of the twentieth century, furnishings became more individualized, reflecting a new stylistic obsession with "art moderne." Function became as important as design and the new garden ornaments were simplified and streamlined. New materials such as mesh, stainless steel, and aluminum replaced the heavier and more ornate earlier materials.

Today anything goes in garden design. People are as apt to use old farm equipment as garden ornaments, as they are to choose neo-classical females, golden Buddhas, Chinese stone lanterns, or old English staddle stones. Materials can be as varied as stone, terra cotta, marble, cast-stone, concrete, cast iron, wrought-iron, wicker, stainless steel, mesh or painted wood. Ornaments can be neo-classical, art deco, or just natural.

And most people who use interior designers realize the importance of a good garden designer. Good gardens don't just happen. They need time, care, and thought. And just as a beautiful garden is not the result of hit-or-miss scattering seeds to the wind, siting garden sculptures and antiques require thoughtful planning. Furnishing a living room requires considerations of scale, size, and style, and so does a formal garden alcove require the same forethought and planning.

It is interesting to note the influence that American pragmatism has had on gardens. It was the American gardener who pioneered wooden garden structures, forgoing the more elaborate stone structures found in Europe. It was the Americans who favored the more durable and cheaper cast iron products. It was Ameri-cans who chose the less expensive molded copies of the classics. And it was Americans who pioneered in an informal outdoor lifestyle.

It is interesting to note that many of today's ornamental garden structures grew out of necessity. Fences and gates kept out marauding animals such as pigs, cows, and deer. Weathervanes and sundials were functional items to tell time and weather. Outbuildings were functional. Walkways were enclosed for weather. Covered patios allowed summer refreshment. Columns and porticos provided protection from weather. Orangeries were built to bring the outside inside.

Environment determined materials. Where trees and forests were abundant, fences and outdoor structures were built of wood. However, in New England and Pennsylvania, native craftsmen were more apt to choose the more abundant fieldstone. Since birds beautified a garden and protected the plants from bugs and insects, gardeners built birdhouses. One can not stress the restorative value of flowing water in a garden and soon every well-appointed garden not only had a flowing fountain, but a birdbath. And soon, classically-inspired gardeners were designing natural looking ponds and pools as garden focal points. Fountains also became garden fixtures, and the flow of water added not just beauty, but soothing sounds.

> Water has always been an important part of garden ornamentation.

19th century Italians were very fond of creating heroic and contrived grottoes, pools, and fancies in their gardens. This particularly elaborate grotto is at the Villa Reale in Italy. The two reclining river gods are inspired by Michelangelo's sculptures of river gods in the Medici Chapel in Florence, Italy.

Chinoiserie, the infatuation with all things Oriental was a popular stylistic design in the early 1800s. A topiary Buddha. *Ladew Topiary Gardens*.

Classic topiary trees, Villa Reale, Italy

One of the most outstanding features of the gardens at Villa Reale is this topiary theatre. A terra cotta figure of Columbine from the Harlequin legend stands ready to perform.

This Dallas, Texas garden is a modern adaptation of a classically inspired design. *Proler/ Oeggerli.*

Mr. Ladew even created a Chinese junk topiary design.

This teahouse was inspired by a teahouse Henry Ladew saw at the Tivoli Gardens.

Cupola, copper and wood, American, early 20th century. *The Garden Antiquary*. $4,000-5,000.

Pricing

It is important to understand what the words "reproduction," "copy," and "antique" mean in the field of garden ornaments and garden furniture. Almost all the seventeenth, eighteenth, and nineteenth century statuary are reproductions or copies of an original. Antique styled chairs, benches, tables, wells, columns, and pedestals are also copied from classic designs. Nineteenth century cast iron furniture was originally mass produced. Early twentieth century sundials, armillaries, and urns were also reproductions based on classic designs.

In the field of garden ornaments, the word "antique" is a relative term when pricing garden art. "Antiques" come in two categories. The high end, which goes for tens of thousands of dollars, includes centuries old classical ruins and works with unusual provenance, which have been a part of classical collections or garden estates. In this book, we use the word "antique" to describe any ornament that dates back to the eighteenth or nineteenth centuries. We use the term "antique" to differentiate and date an item from a twentieth century copy.

We have found that dealers in garden ornaments are a special breed of people. They have all been gracious, helpful, and eager to help us. We thank them for their cooperation. They shared information and helped us with the pricing analysis.

Condition, detail, age, and provenance determine the pricing of an antique garden ornament. However, stylistic and aesthetic considerations also influence collectors. The authors and publishers of this book do not assume any responsibility for any sales or transactions based on information gained from this book.

PART ONE—ARCHITECTURAL ELEMENTS
Chapter 1
Columns

Common materials: marble, vicenza stone, cast stone, wood, and cast iron

In the late nineteenth century, America watched the emergence of a new class of millionaires, the "Robber Barons," who amassed fortunes. In the East, these self-made men made fortunes from investments in the railroads, the oil, steel, and coal industries. In the West, there was money to be made from gold, silver, and cattle. And almost immediately this new monied class adopted opulent lifestyles, building castles, and homes and gardens filled with elaborate ornamental gates, classical statuary, architectural columns, and manicured paths and walkways.

In the eighteenth and nineteenth centuries, wealthy landowners built replicas of Greek and Roman temples and ruins on their land. They brought back architectural remnants from Europe. Many of the wealthier homeowners hired agents to buy European antiques for their gardens. Millionaires such as Frick, Mellon, Carnegie, and the Rockefellers stripped European estates of their art and antiquities. Even well into the twentieth century, it was not unusual to find Greek and Roman columns strewn around gardens of the rich in formalized patterns or an antique Roman river god overlooking a pond or fountain.

These new millionaires had vision and ego, and just as their daring vision amassed incredible fortunes, so did their oversized egoes devise some of the most pretentious and elaborate garden entertainments—labyrinths, puzzling mazes of boxwood, fanciful follies and exotic out-buildings. Gardens soon became the repository of art and classical statuary. Soon American gardeners were planting elaborate avenues and allees of trees, or constructing the arbors, trellises, outdoor patios, and loggias of Italian and Mediterranean villas.

The Dallas Arboretum, Dallas, Texas.

Architectural elements are among the most popular garden ornaments. A private Texas garden. *Proler/Oeggerli.*

Columns define a garden space. *Meadowbloom Gardens, Chester Spring, Pennsylvania.*

Columns add interest to a garden as well as a support for trailing vines. Taormina, Sicily.

It wasn't until the twentieth century that Americans had confidence and appreciation for both American art and American style, and stopped yearning for ancestral pedigrees.

Some of the most popular garden architectural elements found today in American gardens are classic columns with Doric, Ionic, and Corinthian capitals. Columns can either line a road, create a border, or be placed in a haphazard design as an eccentric folly.

Prices begin in the thousands of dollars. Columns sell either singly or as a set. Patina and moss are important to some collectors. Columns with a cleaned surface matter more to other collectors.

18th century Italian stone columns. *Proler/Oeggerli.* $12,000-15,000 a pair.

Patina and moss add to the value. 18th century, Italian, granite gate pier. *Proler/Oeggerli.* $4,500-6,000.

18th century, Rosso Verona, Tuscany columns, Italian. *Proler/ Oeggerli.* $12,000-15,000 a pair.

Right:
Columns, vicenza marble, Italian, circa 1800. A pair of hand-carved vicenza stone finials on a square base, Italian, 19th century, 84-1/2 inches. *Proler/Oeggerli.* $20,000-25,000; $8,000-10,000.

Italian marble columns and a wellhead. *Proler/Oeggerli.*

Trellises add artful accents.

Cast iron Corinthian column, 19th century, American. *Larry Keller, Hobensack and Keller.* $3,000-3,500.

19th century, Italian vicenza stone capital with scrolls, flowers, and acanthus leaves, 19 1/2 inches. *Proler/Oeggerli.* $5,000-7,900 depending on condition.

A 20th century column capital. *Proler/Oeggerli.* $3,000-3,500.

A pair of 18th century Italian clerestory panels. *Proler/Oeggerli.* $15,000-20,000 a pair.

Chapter 2
Finials, Finial Urns

Common materials: marble, cast stone, concrete

Classical finials were usually decorative architectural elements used to top columns, walls, or gates. Today many gardeners prefer to place them free standing on a pedestal as a garden ornament. Finials can be ornate or simple. Carved in high relief with friezes of mythological figures, or simple with egg and dart rims, scalloped, or gadrooned edges, or garlanded with carved ribbons, wreaths, and floral bouquets.

Among the most popular finial styles are ornate hand-carved fruit and flower basket swags. Another popular style is that of the campana urn, a simple form of curved container with or without scrolled handles.

Finials can also be as simple as a round ball or as naturalistic as a carved pineapple, acorn, or stylized flame. They can be one tiered, two tiered, or even three tiered.

One of the most popular forms of finials was the gate pier—a small compact design that fastened to the top of a gate or column.

Sometimes it is hard to tell the difference between a finial and an elaborately carved finial urn. We have defined a finial as an architectural element that does not have a separate top, and a finial urn is an urn with an elaborate lid with its own decorative finial, which is often displayed as a complete unit. We have classified urns with removable elaborately carved lids in chapter 8.

Often garden designers will use an urn both as a finial in the winter and as a planter during the growing season, keeping the cover or lid on in the winter and fall, and filling the bottom container with plants, vines, and flowers in the spring and summer.

Elaborate ornate eighteenth and nineteenth century finials range in price from $400 to $10,000 a pair. Most finials bring higher prices when sold in pairs, than they do when sold singly. However, again condition, design, age, provenance, and aesthetics determine price.

One of the most popular and adaptable forms of garden ornament is the finial.

Villa d'Este.

Middleton Place, Charleston, South Carolina.

Dallas Arboretum, Dallas, Texas.

Finials come in many shapes and styles.

Decorative natural stones make lovely garden ornaments.

Finials can be elaborate or simple such as this unadorned stone finial. 1920s, American. Lanark Manor. $900-1,200.

Stone trough and ball finial. *The Garden Antiquary.* $600-1,000.

Round balls are some of the most popular forms for finials. Valetta, Malta. Similar ball finials have sold at auction for $900-1,500.

Antique French, 19th century gate pier with carved ball finials. *Proler/Oeggerli.* $5,500-6,000 a pair.

Close-up, a ball finial. *The Garden Antiquary.* $800-1,000.

Pineapples were adopted as symbols of hospitality during colonial times.

Pineapples and acorns make lovely garden ornaments.

Antique carved vicenza stone pineapple finials. *Proler/Oeggerli.* $3,000-3,500.

Large antique Italian hand-carved vicenza stone pineapple finial on a square base, 28 inches. *Proler/Oeggerli.* $3,500-4,000.

Villa d'Este, Lake Como, Italy.

Pineapple finials, old and new reproductions, marble, cast stone and poured concrete, American. *Hobensack and Keller.* $100-200.

Two antique pineapple finials, hand-carved Italian vicenza stone on square bases, antique, 28 inches. *Proler/Oeggerli.* $7,500-8,000 a pair.

Antique, Italian finial with a classical design. *Proler/Oeggerli.* $3,000-3,500.

The everlasting light has been a symbol of life after death throughout history. Often flame finials were found on funerary objects.

A French flame-shaped stone finial. *Proler/ Oeggerli.* $5,000-7,000 a pair.

A pair of 18th century French pink granite finials from a castle in Reims in the Champagne region of France, 39 inches tall. *Proler/ Oeggerli.* $12,500-15,000 a pair.

One of a pair of limestone, flame finial urns with removable lids, European, late 19th century. *The Garden Antiquary.* $5,000-6,000 for the pair.

19th century hand-carved vicenza stone urns with finial tops. *Proler/Oeggerli.* $3,000-4,000.

Old Westbury Gardens, Old Westbury, Long Island, New York.

Below:
Antique hand-carved Italian vicenza stone scalloped finial urn on pedestal, 43-1/2 inches. *Proler/ Oeggerli.* $7,000-10,000 a pair.

A pair of stylized, glazed terra cotta finials, French, 19th century. *The Garden Antiquary.* $2,000-3,000 the pair.

34

19th century, vicenza stone finial urns with a carved fruit basket swag finial, egg and dart trimmed rims, sides are mounted with scrolled handles and carved with panels of acanthus leaves, 40 inches. *Proler/Oeggerli.* $7,000-10,000.

An antique monumental, Italian hand-carved vicenza stone finial resting on a square pedestal. The sides and top are decorated with lion heads, medallions, and draped with swags and garlands. A carved flower finial is mounted on the top, 63 inches. *Proler/Oeggerli.* $18,000-20,000 a pair.

Villa d'Este, Lake Como, Italy.

19th century Italian vicenza stone gate pier finial. *Proler/Oeggerli.* $5,000-6,000.

19th century Italian vicenza stone gate pier finial with fruit and flower basket swag on top. *Proler/Oeggerli.* $8,000-10,500.

Italian vicenza stone gate pier finial. *Proler/Oeggerli.* $5,000-6,000.

Villa d'Este, Lake Como, Italy.

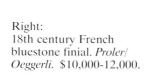

Right:
18th century French bluestone finial. *Proler/Oeggerli.* $10,000-12,000.

Private garden in Texas. *Proler/Oeggerli.*

Detail.

37

One of a pair of antique neo-classical style hand-carved vicenza stone finials with removable tops. The sides are carved with classical figures. The bases are encircled with ribbon-tied berries and laurel leaves on a rising circular foot and square base. *Proler/Oeggerli.* $15,000-20,000 a pair.

Elaborate hand-carved vicenza stone finial urn with fruit basket swag, ribbon garlanded base. *Proler/Oeggerli.* $8,000-12,000 a pair.

Reverse of above.

Similar carved stone obelisk finials have sold at auction for $2,000-6,000. Villa d'Este, Lake Como, Italy.

One of a pair of composition stone obelisk finials. *The Garden Antiquary.* $5,000-6,000 for the pair.

An antique hand-carved Italian vicenza stone fruit and flower finial decorated with scrolls and scalloped bases, 39 inches. *Proler/Oeggerli.* $7,000-8,500.

19th century antique Italian hand-carved vicenza stone fruit and flower basket finial. *Proler/Oeggerli.* $7,000-8,000.

Detail.

Italian vicenza stone fruit and flower basket swag finial. *Proler/Oeggerli.* $7,000-8,000 a pair.

Italian vicenza stone fruit basket finial. *Proler/Oeggerli.* $5,000-6,000 a pair.

19th century Italian vicenza stone flower basket. *Proler/Oeggerli.* $5,500-6,500 a pair.

19th century Italian vicenza stone flower basket. *Proler/Oeggerli.* $7,000-8,000 a pair.

19th century limestone finial fruit compotes. *Anthony Garden Boutique.* $3,000-4,500.

19th century cast stone fruit basket compotes. *Anthony Garden Boutique.* $3,000-5,000 a pair.

19th century fruit basket swag. *Ladew Topiary Gardens*.

A private garden in Dallas, Texas. *Proler/Oeggerli.*

Palm Beach, Florida.

A private garden in Dallas, Texas. *Proler/Oeggerli.*

Highly carved stone finial urn.

Lanark Manor.

Top left and left:
A private garden in
Westchester, New York.
The Garden Antiquary.

Finial Urns

Proler/Oeggerli.

Italian vicenza stone urn with gadrooned body resting on lotus leaves. The acorn finial is removable, 39 inches. *Proler/Oeggerli.* $7,500.

Stone urn. *Proler/Oeggerli.*

Close-up of carved Italian urn.

One of a pair of hand-carved Italian vicenza stone finial urns with gadrooning on lotus leaves, 26 inches. *Proler/Oeggerli.* $9,700 a pair.

One of a pair of antique Italian neo-classical vicenza stone urns on square bases, 43 inches. *Proler/Oeggerli.* $10,000-12,000 a pair.

Chapter 3
Statuary

Common materials: marble, vicenza stone, cast stone, limestone, sandstone, terra cotta

One has only to look at the excavated ruins of the gardens of Pompeii to trace the roots of modern garden design and ornamentation. Ruined fountains, columns, statuary, sundials, and carefully laid stone paths surround the private villas of these long gone Romans.

Their influence remains today and has influenced gardeners for hundreds of years. One of the first praises to be recorded in modern history about the ancient Greek and Roman garden designs was expressed in 1713 by Alexander Pope when he praised "the taste of the ancients in their gardens."

However, a high regard for the ancients began in earnest in the eighteenth century when travelers to Italy first experienced the beauty of the Italian gardens. More and more English and French traveled to Italy and returned with purchases of ancient statuary, installing these antiques both inside and outside their homes. And soon garden designers were using this statuary to ornament their gardens.

By the eighteenth century, these Italian models influenced the New World, and many of the Southern landed gentry also returned from first-time visits to Italy, wide-eyed and covetous, ready to copy the Italian ideas in their own gardens.

Capability Brown, who was one of the most famous early English garden designers in the eighteenth century, was one of the few who was not impressed by the Italianate formality and artificiality. Brown believed in romantic gardens and chose to use natural paths, bridges, and plantings, not statuary, in his garden designs. But by the nineteenth century, more and more gardeners were intrigued by the Italianate form and began to design contrived environments filled with imaginative excess such as siting ancient ruins, distressed grottoes, and eccentric follies all crowned with at least one Roman river god, Zeus, Neptune, or a nude Venus.

Georgian England liked classical lines and an ordered symmetry. Soon gardens had sets of the four seasons, the five senses, and male and female gardeners.

One of a set of four seasons. Middleton Place, Charleston, South Carolina.

The Victorians decorated their furniture with animal imagery. They installed lions on everything, as legs and supports for tables, chairs, and settees. They favored gargoyles and ferocious heads and claws as wall plaques and decorations. In their wall hangings and fabrics, they also favored an artificial and stylized natural design of contrived exotic flowers, vines, and landscapes.

So it was no surprise to see that their passion for structure and organization resulted in rigid plantings, the use of mass produced ornate cast iron furniture, and seating with stylized renditions of natural imagery, and mass produced terra cotta, zinc, and cast iron statuary of animal figures.

One of the most popular nineteenth century statuary conceits was the common appearance of matching pairs of male and female gardeners as well as naked cherubs gamboling on lawns and gracing fountains. Eagles were particularly popular in America. Foo Dogs became a symbol of the mysterious Orient.

Among the most popular materials used were marble and stone. By the middle of the nineteenth century, terra cotta and cast iron became popular choices. By the late nineteenth century, manufacturers were producing cast iron, zinc, and lead statuary. In the nineteenth century, a growing interest in the study of archeology and the classics continued, and, as scholars expanded their study to Rome, Greece, and Ancient Egypt, classical copies and figures began to appear in gardens of all sizes.

Old Westbury Gardens, the former Phipps Estate.

The grand allee of the Villa Torrigiani, Lucca, Italy.

Nothing is more inviting than a well-placed garden sculpture. A keyhole arbor at the Ladew Topiary Gardens.

Or more fun than the element of surprise. Lanark Manor, Lanark, Pennsylvania.

This trend towards copycating European gardens was the motivation for the development of garden design in America. And no where was this more evident in the choice of garden statuary. American gardens were filled with classical groupings of the four seasons, the five senses, and the muses of art and literature.

But beginning in the late nineteenth century, realism took hold of the Victorian fancies and soon the landed gentry's obsession with the hunt began to show itself and gardens became populated by cast iron, lead and stone stags, dogs, lions, and eagles. Even today a greyhound or a whippet can be found casually located at garden entrances in suburban gardens, and the proliferation of painted stone deer in backyards is becoming a common sight in many suburban "estates."

One of the most extraordinary hunt displays is the topiary hunt scene of two riders, their hounds, and a very frightened fox on the grounds of the Ladew Topiary Gardens in Monkton, Maryland.

A fascination for the past remains today. In fact visiting the lush gardens of the eighteenth century villas of Italy, one finds a surfeit of the classical past. Gardens and grounds are filled with marble and stone, Greek and Roman Gods, particularly Zeus, Neptune, Diana, Venus, Pan, Bacchus, as well as hordes of nymphs, cherubs, and angelic putti.

Antique statues such as this classical Greek figure have been prized by collectors. Togaed Roman figure, marble, 2nd century, A.D. *The Garden Antiquary.* $100,000-120,000.

The four seasons have been popular garden ornaments since classical times. Usually the four seasons are represented by four classically robed women. However, cherubs or putti also represent the seasons. Usually Spring holds a basket or garland of flowers, Summer holds wheat, Fall holds grapes, and Winter holds a flame.

Spring.

Summer.

Detail of Fall holding a bunch of grapes.

Fall.

18th century, vicenza stone, garland draped female nude. *Proler/Oeggerli.* $25,000-30,000.

One particularly interesting exception can be found in the Villa Reale di Marlia, outside of Lucca, where a complete topiary theatre set features the familiar commedia dell' arte figures of Harlequin, Punchinello, and Columbine, the Italian ancestors of the better-known English Punch and Judy shows.

Throughout our visits to formal American gardens we have still found that the most popular garden figures are female nudes, the classically-gowned female figures, nude cherubs, and heroic males. And the most popular fountain ornaments are river gods masks, heroic lions, and Bacchus look-a-likes.

Another example of Summer holding the harvest. A magnificent and rare matched set of Italian hand-modeled terra cotta figures of the four seasons with matching pedestals, early 20th century, 60 inches. *Proler/Oeggerli.* $25,000-30,000 a set.

Spring. *Proler/Oeggerli.*

Pricing

Good quality antique statuary can range in price from $2,000 to $20,000. Good quality twentieth century reproductions can cost as little as a few hundred dollars. Sets of the four seasons or the five senses can be priced for more than $10,000. Single pieces can cost as little as $1,000. Good quality nineteenth century lead garden figures can cost between $10,000 and $15,000.

Again, prices are determined by age, condition, aesthetics, subject matter, and provenance. Female nudes bring in higher prices than male nudes. Classical figures still are more popular than contemporary figures. Cherubs, putti, and angels still retain their appeal. Dogs, stags, and eagles are particularly appealing to American collectors.

Among the most widely copied Renaissance works appearing as garden art are Michelangelo's *David* and his river gods from the Medici Chapel. Both originals can be found in Florence. Andrea del Verocchio's 1478 statue of a young boy with a dolphin has also been copied as a popular fountain sculpture.

Famous nineteenth century terra cotta sculptors are Englishmen Mark Blanchard, John Marriott Blashfield, and Coade and Sealey. One of the best-known American cast iron makers was J.W. Fiske of New York City.

In 1839, Mark Blanchard, who had served his apprenticeship with Coade and Sealey, set up his own terra cotta works in England. It is known that he bought some of Coade's molds and used them as models.

John Marriott Blashfield (1830-1870) set up his own terra cotta works in 1851 after the Great Exhibition. He also made outstanding terra cotta figures.

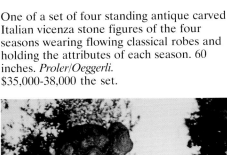

One of a set of four standing antique carved Italian vicenza stone figures of the four seasons wearing flowing classical robes and holding the attributes of each season. 60 inches. *Proler/Oeggerli.* $35,000-38,000 the set.

Winter holding the flame. Two antique Italian hand-carved vicenza stone female statues wearing classical robes, one holding a flame, the other a bunch of wheat, on matching pedestals. 63 inches. *Proler/Oeggerli.* $9,000-10,700.

Summer holding the sheaves of wheat showing the harvest. These statues usually sell in sets or $12,000-15,000 each. *Proler/Oeggerli.*

Spring holding a basket of flowers.
Proler/Oeggerli.

Antique Italian hand-carved vicenza stone female statues wearing classical robes, holding a flame and sheaf of wheat from an other view. *Proler/Oeggerli.*

18th and 19th century Italian villas such as Villa Reale near Lucca, in village of Marlia, had marvelous garden designs with an abundance of antique statuary of Greek, Roman, and mythological figures.

Statuary from the front lawn of Villa Reale, Marlia, Italy. Statuary like this has sold at auction for $5,000-10,000 depending on age, condition, and detail.

A series of four sandstone/limestone English reproductions of the four seasons based on an original 18th or 19th century mold. *Hobensack and Keller.* About $1,250 each.

Eighteenth century society enjoyed masquerade balls and dressing as rustics. The fashionable ladies of the day would dress as milkmaids, shepherdesses, flower girls, and characters from the commedia dell' arte. The concept of an ideal rural Arcadia remained popular through the Victorian age. Lead garden figures in 18th century dress were popular as garden ornaments through the early 20th century. These figures have sold at auction for $10,000-15,000.

Mabel and John Ringling Museum, Sarasota, Florida.

Below:
19th century lead garden figure. *Ladew Topiary Gardens.*

19th century lead garden figure. *Ladew Topiary Gardens.* Note the 18th century dress.

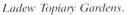

Ladew Topiary Gardens.

19th century lead garden figure from the Ladew Topiary Gardens. Generally these lead figures sell for $2,000-3,000, except when the statue has provenance from a famous garden. Age and detail also determine price.

A pair of lead standing male and female figures, American, early 20th century. *The Garden Antiquary*. $6,000-7,500 for the pair.

A portrait bust on a pedestal with a gargoyle bust head. Old Westbury Gardens, Old Westbury, New York.

Old Westbury Gardens.

Old Westbury Gardens.

57

Left:
Musical putti have also been popular garden sculptures. Old Westbury Gardens.

Right:
Terra cotta figure of Punchinello. Villa Reale, Marlia, Italy.

Below left:
Carved marble Bacchus, probably 1910-1920. This form of statue is called a *term* because it only shows the shoulders and not the full figure. A close-up of the female companion piece is also shown at right. *Larry Keller.* $10,000-12,000 a pair.

Left:
One of a pair of lead garden figures, early 20th century, American. *Larry Keller*. $1,200-1,500 a pair.

Right:
Detail showing his spade.

Left:
Matching female figure. *Larry Keller*.

Right:
Detail showing her basket of flowers.

St. Fiacre, the saint of gardeners, American, 20th century, probably 1930s. This piece has great patina, and is signed Urkins Studio, NYC. *Larry Keller*.

Stone angels have become one of the most common garden ornaments. This is a vintage one. Price is determined by size and age. $75-200.

Right:
A white marble bust of a young Italian noble woman carved by one of the most popular portrait sculptors of his day, Scottish-born Lawrence MacDonald (1799-1878.) Italian aristocracy vied for the privilege of being portrayed by MacDonald during his extended stay in Rome, 30 inches. *Proler/Oeggerli.* $6,000-7,500.

Sculptures add focal points in even the most elaborate garden. Tulip time at Keukenhof Gardens, Holland.

An early American lead female figure. *Larry Keller*.

An unusual marble figure of Adam and Eve, 19th century, American. *Ladew Topiary Gardens*. Similar statues have sold at auction for $8,000-12,000.

Left:
Michelangelo's *David* in Florence is perhaps the most famous male nude, and one of the most copied. The original is in the Galleria Accademia in Florence. A copy (*pictured*) stands in the Piazza Signorina in Florence, Italy.

Left:
19th century vicenza stone copy of the famous Renaissance statue. *Proler/Oeggerli.* $22,000-28,000.

Right:
Male nudes are not as popular as females. This one reclines against a tree trunk. Statue of David, composition stone, American, early 20th century. *The Garden Antiquary.*

Villa d'Este.

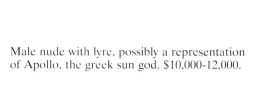

Male nude with lyre, possibly a representation of Apollo, the greek sun god. $10,000-12,000.

Antique standing male nude. *Proler/Oeggerli.*

18th century hand-carved vicenza stone statue of a woman with a child. *Proler/ Oeggerli.* $25,000-27,500.

19th century Italian, vicenza stone torso of a Roman centurion. *Proler/ Oeggerli.* $7,500-8,500.

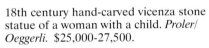

Antique Italian hand-carved vicenza stone bust of Janus, 32 inches. *Proler/Oeggerli.* $5,500-6,500.

19th century Italian vicenza stone, standing cherub holding a fish. *Proler/Oeggerli.* $4,500-5,000.

Young children, putti, and cherubs have always been popular ornaments.

20th century cast stone musical putto playing the pipes. *Ladew Topiary Gardens.*

One of a pair of 20th century musical fauns. One is turned to the right. The other faces the left. Each plays an instrument: one a tambourine, the other cymbals. The base is an acanthus leaf, decorated carved pedestal. Statuary often came in pairs or sets representing the four seasons, the five senses, the muses, etc. *Ladew Topiary Gardens.* Similar fauns have sold for auction for $2,500-5,000.

20th century musical cast stone putto playing tambourines. *Ladew Topiary Gardens.*

Ladew Topiary Gardens.

A pair of Italian hand-carved vicenza stone putti. *Proler/Oeggerli.*

Proler/Oeggerli.

67

An important set of antique hand-carved stone putti of the four
seasons resting on matching carved scrolled bases. 32 inches.
Proler/Oeggerli. $9,500-10,500 the set.

Antique 19th century Italian hand-carved
vicenza stone putto with wings, a pillow
and blanket over his head. 30 inches.
Proler/Oeggerli. $5,000-6,500.

A 19th century hand-carved Italian vicenza stone cherub leaning upon a tree trunk, holding up bunches of grapes. This piece comes from the Tuscany region of Italy. 30 inches. *Proler/Oeggerli.* $6,000-6,500.

Detail.

One of a pair of antique French hand-carved stone putti with grapes, sitting on a wine jug, 32 inches. This is a popular classical image and has often been reproduced. *Proler/Oeggerli.* $8,000-9,000.

Left:
A modern cast stone figure of Bacchus. *Proler/Oeggerli.* $2,500-3,500.

Below left:
Early French 18th century hand-carved stone bust of a warrior, 26 inches. *Proler/ Oeggerli.* $2,500-3,400.

Standing figure of a saint. *Hobensack and Keller.*

This hunt scene is the signature
of Ladew Topiary Gardens.

The Pondhouse.

These concrete cranes were popular garden and pool ornaments in the 1920s. They are now very popular and sell from $200-500 depending on condition, pose, and age.

Gates at Villa Reale.

Modern molded putti. *Hobensack and Keller*. $100-300.

Stags were popular 19th century French and English garden ornaments. Victorian society especially liked the idea of recreating rural scenes in their interior and garden designs. Their furniture had ornate carved animal legs and arms, and animal designs on their fabrics.

Stag, Zinc, American made, circa 19th century. This piece came from the Butcher estate in Chestnut Hill, Pennsylvania. It may have been made by the J. W. Fiske foundry. It is very unusual to find a zinc statue in such good condition. *Hobensack and Keller.* $5,000-6,500.

Stag statue by Barye, cast bronze, French, 19th century. *The Garden Antiquary.* $14,500-16,000.

Greyhounds have also been
popular garden ornaments.
Lanark Manor.

Cast iron whippet, American,
mid-20th century. *Hobensack
and Keller*.
$1,750-2,000.

Cast stone golden horse. *The Garden Antiquary.*

Cast stone horse. *The Garden Antiquary.*

A cast stone horse. *The Garden Antiquary.*

A cast iron eagle statue. Ladew Topiary Gardens.
Similar pieces have sold at auction for $5,000-8,000.

Eagle, zinc, American, c. 1880, signed and dated J.W. Fiske, New
York. *The Garden Antiquary*. $23,000-26,000.

Detail.

One of a pair of cement eagles, American, 20th century. *The
Garden Antiquary*. $750-900 for the pair.

A 20th century cast stone squirrel.
Ladew Topiary Gardens.

Female *Sower* statue, zinc, 19th century, French.
The Garden Antiquary. $4,500-5,500.

The Beck garden.

Chapter 4
Masks, Grotesques, Lions, Sphinxes, Wall Plaques

Common materials: marble, vicenza stone, cast stone, limestone, sandstone, terra cotta

One can't explain the extraordinary fascination with mythological creatures such as sphinxes, griffins, gargoyles, and dragons throughout history. But these mythological creatures can be found adorning European cathedrals, castles, palaces, and city halls.

Napoleon introduced the Egyptian sphinx into European design in the early nineteenth century, and soon it became an important design element appearing in both interiors and exteriors on furniture, in gardens, and as watch guards outside gates and steps.

One of a pair of carved stone sphinxes, in the form of a woman dressed in 18th century court dress, French, 40 inches. *Proler/Oeggerli.* $8,000-8,700 a pair.

Details of the carving.

Villa Reale.

Villa Reale.

Two sphinx from Old
Westbury Gardens.
Similar ones have sold
for $10,000-15,000 at
auction.

19th century, white Carrara marble sphinx with a cherub resting on its back, 60 inches. The originals are in Versailles. $35,000-40,000.

Mabel and John Ringling Museum, Sarasota, Florida.

Perhaps it is because he is known as the "King of the beasts" that the lion has been regarded as a symbol of royalty for many centuries. And throughout Europe one finds this animal as a ubiquitous symbol of royalty and might. Heraldic lions holding family, royal and city crests appear everywhere—on castles, city halls, city gates, cathedrals, and private homes. Lions have been particularly popular since Gothic times as ornaments for both furniture and architecture.

Collectors particularly like heroic lions standing guard on walls, before gates, and by themselves, and collect lions because of their stance, the detail of their manes, their gaze, and their pose.

Foo Dogs have been a popular symbol in China for hundreds of centuries, but have become a recent phenomenon in Europe and America only within the last one hundred and fifty years. One can trace their appearance to a renewed interest in the Orient. Foo Dogs usually come in pairs symbolizing power and fertility. The female usually has a young cub under her paw, while the male holds a globe of the world. Foo Dogs have highly stylized features and manes.

Lion heads, carved marble, American, early 20th century. *The Garden Antiquary*. $4,000-4,500 for the four.

Fountain Masks

Two small antique Italian hand-carved vicenza stone lion fountain masks, 12 inches. *Proler/Oeggerli*. $1,200-1,500.

Two Italian vicenza stone lion fountain masks and one French stone putto fountain mask, 12 inches. *Proler/Oeggerli.* $1,000-1,200 each.

Villa Reale. The gardens of Villa Reale were created in the 17th and 18th centuries. In 1805 it became the home of Napoleon's sister Elisa. Today it is privately owned and is open to the public.

Above and left: Antique, Italian hand-carved vicenza stone grotesque fountain mask, 17 inches. *Proler/Oeggerli.* $1,700-1,900.

Antique Italian, hand-carved, vicenza stone grotesque fountain mask, 17 inches high. *Proler/Oeggerli.* $1,700-1,900.

Antique Italian hand-carved vicenza stone grotesque fountain mask, 15 inches. $2,000-2,500.

Antique Italian, hand-carved, vicenza stone, square grotesque fountain mask, 16 inches high. *Proler/Oeggerli.* $2,000-2,300.

Antique Italian hand-carved vicenza stone fountain mask with scrolls and Bacchus, 16 inches. *Proler/Oeggerli.* $1,700-1,900.

River god.

Lion head.

Stylized grotesque.

Satyr.

85

Antique, Italian, hand-carved vicenza stone, fountain masks. *Proler/Oeggerli.* $1,700-1,900.

Top left:
One of a pair of unusual carved stone Foo Dog. American, 20th century. Foo Dogs are stylized lion/dogs and came in pairs. The male held a globe of the world under his paw symbolizing power. The female held a cub under her paw symbolizing fertility and life. *The Garden Antiquary*. $17,500 for the pair.

Top right:
Lions with royal crests have been found on buildings since the Renaissance. This lion adorns a gate in Valetta, Malta.

Bottom:
This lion adorns a pillar in the Piazza Signorina in Florence, Italy.

A 20th century cast stone lion.

Lions. Valetta, Malta.

Anthony Garden Boutique. $4,000-4,500.

A 20th century cast stone lion.

A 20th century cast stone lion.

Hand-carved Italian vicenza stone carved lion. *Proler/Oeggerli.* $5,000-8,000 a pair.

19th century, Italian hand-carved vicenza stone lions supporting an armorial shield with the crest of Florence in each paw, 24 inches. *Proler/Oeggerli.* $9,000-10,000 a pair.

90

A pair of 30-inch high antique hand-carved vicenza stone lions modeled after lions sculpted by Antonio Canova (1757-1822). The originals can be found on Canova's monument of Pope Clement XIII in St. Peter's Basilica in Rome, Italy. *Proler/Oeggerli.* $8,000-8,500 a pair.

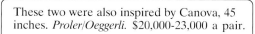

These two were also inspired by Canova, 45 inches. *Proler/Oeggerli.* $20,000-23,000 a pair.

Late 19th century, Italian vicenza stone lions, 70 inches. *Proler/Oeggerli.* $40,000-43,000 a pair.

Above and right:
Two antique Italian hand-carved vicenza stone lions with their heads turned sideways, 36 inches. *Proler/Oeggerli.* $10,000-12,000 a pair.

Standing lion, 43 inches. *Proler/Oeggerli.* $20,000-25,000.

Below:
One of a pair of Italian vicenza stone lions with the crest of Florence, Italy. *Proler/Oeggerli.* $9,000-10,000 a pair.

Lion fountain mask. *Proler/Oeggerli.* $1,700-1,900.

20th century fountain mask. *Hobensack and Keller.* $300-400.

Early 20th century Chinese Foo Dogs. $300-500 a pair.

A pair of oversized cast stone Foo Dogs, mid 20th century. It is unusual to find these dogs in such a large size and with such scale. *Hobensack and Keller.* $4,500-5,000 a pair.

Detail.

19th century English stoneware cornucopia in the form of a bearded man. *Proler/Oeggerli.* $7,500.

Old Westbury Gardens.

Old Westbury Gardens.

Wall Plaques

Antique, hand-carved vicenza stone carved lion head wall plaque. *Proler/Oeggerli.*

Antique hand-carved lion wall plaque medallion. *Proler/Oeggerli.*

Vicenza stone wall plaque in the form of a flower. *Proler/Oeggerli.* $1,200.

Antique 18th century hand-carved Venetian marble wall plaque showing the St. Mark's lion, with the insignia of Venice, 34 inches. *Proler/Oeggerli.* $7,200.

Italian antique hand-carved stone wall plaque showing the Madonna and child, 22 inches. *Proler/Oeggerli.* $2,000-2,500.

Proler/Oeggerli.

97

PART TWO—FUNCTIONAL OBJECTS
Chapter 5
Birdbaths, Birdhouses

Common materials: wood, stone, marbles, cast iron

For many centuries raising doves and pigeons was a popular hobby and it is not unusual to find a formal dovecote on eighteenth and nineteenth century estates. Farmers knew that birds ate destructive bugs and insects. They also propagate wildflower seeds. So the origins of birdbaths and birdhouses can be traced to both pragmatic and decorative origins.

Aesthetically, birds are lovely creatures to watch and offer many fascinating seasonal displays. Who hasn't been amazed at the dexterous mating displays of the male bird? Or awed by the determined energy of their earnest nest building? Or thrilled by the beauty of their spring and summer plumage?

Birdbaths not only attract birds, they provide a lovely focal point for a garden. Most birdbaths are basins set atop carved pedestals.

Birdhouses are a more recent garden ornament and have often inspired extravagant architecture. Wren houses are usually small cottages. Dovecotes appear as monumental towers, and purple martin birdhouses have the look of condominiums. But most of all, bird garden ornaments, whether simple or complex, have a widespread appeal as both romantic and eccentric fantasies.

Pricing of birdbaths is varied. Again, condition, age, material, and aesthetics influence price. Antique birdbaths range in price from $800 to $2,000. Folk art birdhouses can cost as much as $900.

BIRDBATHS

Birdbaths have long been a popular garden focal point with both a functional and decorative intent.

Boone Hall, Charleston, South Carolina

Middleton Place, Charleston, South Carolina.

Antique French hand-carved white marble birdbath with round top on baluster pedestal decorated with acanthus leaves, 37 inches. *Proler/ Oeggerli.* $11,700.

An antique hand-carved vicenza stone birdbath with a gadrooned bowl supported by a fluted pedestal, decorated with acanthus leaves, 40 inches. *Proler/Oeggerli.* $6,700.

A decorative antique hand-carved vicenza stone oval birdbath. The rim has a carved rope design and masks in high relief. The sides are carved with ribbons and fruit swags supported by a rising fluted oval base. 28 inches. *Proler/Oeggerli.* $7,900.

An antique hand-carved oval Italian vicenza stone birdbath with shallow gadrooned basin supported on a pedestal carved with two intertwined stylized dolphins. 18 inches. *Proler/Oeggerli.* $5,800.

Antique, 19th century, vicenza stone, Italian, center bird-bath, with a carved pedestal, its basin is decorated with a scalloped egg and dart pattern. Its base has carved acanthus leaves. 28 inches. *Proler/Oeggerli.* $6,000-6,800.

Cast stone birdbaths. *Hobensack and Keller.* $250-500.

101

19th century, American cast stone birdbath with a pedestal base carved as a tree trunk. *Anthony Garden Boutique*. $3,000-3,500.

Birdbath, composition stone, 20th century, English reproduction. *The Garden Antiquary*. $550.

Monika Doman.

Chapter 6
Sundials, Armillary Globes

Common materials: marble, cast stone, concrete

How do you tell time? Today few of us can live without a watch. And yet early in our civilization one of the ways to tell time was to follow the sun and trace its shadows to determine the passing of time. Formally designed sundials can be seen still standing in Pompeii, and amazingly the style and design has changed little. A sundial is a flat semi-circular surface with a bronze or cast iron arrow, called a gnomen. It is the shadow from the gnomen that tells the time.

Originally, a sundial had to be calibrated so that it could accurately tell the time of the region. It also had to be positioned correctly to catch the rays of the sun. Today sundials have long lost their functional duties, but remain popular as garden ornaments. Antique sundials range in price from $1,000 to $2,000. However, unusual designs can command much higher prices.

Middleton Place, Charleston, South Carolina.

19th century Italian
vicenza stone semi-
circular bench in the
Roman style with a
vicenza stone pedestal;
an armillarial sundial in
the middle. *Proler/
Oeggerli.* Bench: $20,000.
Armillary: $6,500.

19th century Italian, vicenza stone sundial with four masks and a
flower swag decoration and a bronze sundial plate. *Proler/Oeggerli.*
$14,500.

Antique Italian sundial. *Proler/Oeggerli.*
$3,000.

Cast iron gnomon of a sundial on a concrete platform. *Proler/ Oeggerli.* Sundials: $2,500-3,000.

Antique, Italian, carved vicenza stone wall sundial. *Proler/Oeggerli.* $3,000.

Two Italian vicenza stone neo-classical sundial wall plaques: one with a circle design insert, the other with a star. 24 inches. *Proler/ Oeggerli.* $3,900 each.

These are all Italian vicenza stone neo-classical sundial wall plaques, 24 inches. *Proler/Oeggerli.* $2,500-3,000.

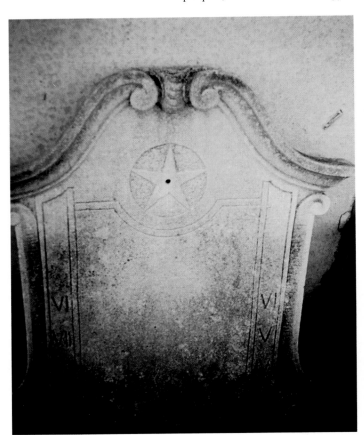

Modern sundial on a pedestal. *Hobensack and Keller*. $500.

A modern sundial plate. $150.

Sandstone sundial, mid-19th century, 33 inches. *Hobensack and Keller*. $5,200.

Armillary Globes

Common materials: bronze, cast iron, wrought iron

Armillaries traditionally were used as navigational and time devices. Like a sundial, they had to be properly calibrated so that they would function correctly. Today armillaries are mainly ornamental. They consist of a bronze or cast iron globe that has been inscribed with numbers and rests on a pedestal. Antique armillaries can range in price from $3,000 to $4,000.

Late 19th century armillary, American. *Anthony Garden Boutique.* $4,000.

Late 19th century armillary, American. *Anthony Garden Boutique.* $3,500-4,000.

Chapter 7
Fountains

Common materials: marble, cast stone, vicenza stone, concrete, cast iron, wrought iron

Fountains have been an important garden focal point since the seventeenth century. Water has always enhanced gardens, adding a splash of light, a soothing sound, and a graceful focal point. There are three different fountain styles: wall fountains with a spouting mask, a one, two, or multi-tiered center fountain, or a simple basin. Common styles of fountain spouts are fish, birds, dolphins, cranes, as well as male river god masks, lion heads, and even graceful maidens. Renaissance fountains are known for their elaborate carvings. The Victorians loved elaborate cast iron creations. Today many gardeners prefer a more simple, stylized fount of water.

One of the most popular Renaissance statues, Andrea del Verocchio's winged putto holding a dolphin, has been one of the most copied and best loved figures and can be found in gardens of every scale. Another popular figure has been Estelle Barretto Parsons' cast bronze *Laughing Boy with Turtles*.

Water is always a decorative garden feature. Villa Reale, Italy.

Ladew Topiary Gardens.

A Dallas garden swimming pool.
Proler/Oeggerli.

Grottoes are common features in 17th and 18th century gardens. Villa Reale, Marlia, Italy.

A three-tiered Victorian fountain as seen through an arbor in Ladew Topiary Gardens.

One of the fountains in the gardens of the Dallas Arboretum.

Dallas Arboretum, Dallas, Texas.

A wall fountain in a garden alcove in a private garden in Dallas. *Proler/Oeggerli.*

Above and right:
An impressive hand-carved Italian two-tiered vicenza stone center fountain. The two bowls are raised on a square base with four stylized dolphin waterspouts and surmounted by a flower finial. 90 inches. $38,000.

Swimming pools add special accents to a garden.

An antique Italian wellhead that is now a fountain. *Proler/Oeggerli.*

Detail of armorial shield on side.

Antique hand-carved Italian vicenza stone basin with a choice of lion or dolphin waterspout. The gadrooned bowl is supported on a baluster-shaped pedestal with a lion fountain mask. It is also found with a stylized dolphin waterspout. 32 inches. *Proler/ Oeggerli.* $7,900.

Left and below:
Beautiful hand-carved Italian vicenza stone center fountain with two playful cherubs sitting on a round rock base and holding up a shell waterspout. *Proler/ Oeggerli.* $12,000-25,000.

20th century fountain. *Meadowbloom Gardens.*

French center fountain, round pedestal, cherub with a swan waterspout, 14 inches. *Proler/Oeggerli.* $2,500-3,000.

Rare Italian antique hand-carved vicenza stone neo-classical wall fountain with a backplate, surround and bowl on stand and a pool. 66 inches. *Proler/Oeggerli.* $10,000-12,500.

19th century, hand-carved vicenza stone Italian wall fountain on a volute stand with stepped base. The scrolled backplate is carved with shells and lion mask waterspout; the sloping shallow rectangular gadrooned bowl is carved with scrolls. 50 inches high. *Proler/Oeggerli.* $9,000-10,000.

A tall and decorative antique hand-carved vicenza stone wall fountain. The shell-shaped bowl is on a scrolled pedestal surmounted by a stylized dolphin waterspout. 73 inches. *Proler/Oeggerli.* $10,000-12,200.

A small decorative antique hand-carved vicenza stone wall fountain with stylized dolphin waterspout supported on an ornamental style clamshell with undulating sides and circular base. *Proler/Oeggerli.* $7,000-8,000.

Antique hand-carved vicenza stone center fountain with baluster pedestal supporting a round bowl decorated with floral design. 39 inches. *Proler/Oeggerli.* $8,200-9,500.

Hand-carved Italian vicenza stone wall fountain on stand with gadrooned bowl and backplate in serpentine form with scrolls and stylized flower waterspout. Early 20th century, 65 inches. *Proler/Oeggerli.* $9,700-11,000.

Antique Italian hand-carved white Verona marble and vicenza stone half octagonal wall fountain. The 18th century marble pool surround carved with inset panels is attached to the 19th century vicenza stone backplate with scalloped rim and grotesque fountain mask. 10 feet. *Proler/Oeggerli.* $45,000-49,000.

Hand-carved vicenza stone wall fountain with gadrooned bowl and backplate in serpentine form with stylized flower and leaves. Italian, early 20th century, 70 inches. *Proler/Oeggerli.* $9,500.

Hand-carved vicenza stone wall fountain with a gadrooned bowl carved with ribbon-tied swags. The backplate in semi-circular form with a carved mask. Italy, early 20th century, 65 inches. *Proler/Oeggerli.* $8,500.

19th century, hand-carved vicenza stone wall fountain on a stand, the backplate with scrolls and grotesque mask waterspout. 49 inches. *Proler/Oeggerli.* $10,000-12,000.

Top left:
Hand-carved Italian vicenza stone wall fountain on stand, the backplate with scrolls and lion mask waterspout. 55 inches. *Proler/Oeggerli.* $6,500-7,500.

Top right:
French 19th century limestone wall fountain. *Proler/Oeggerli.* $12,000-15,000.

Bottom:
Hand-carved recreation of a French 17th century Louis XIV limestone wall fountain with classical river god mask. 69 inches. *Proler/Oeggerli.*

A recreation of a French 17th century Louis XIV limestone wall fountain with a elaborate scroll design and river god mask. 78 inches. $10,000-12,700. *Proler/Oeggerli.* $12,000-13,500.

Hand-carved recreation of a French 18th century limestone fountain on stand with putto fountain mask. 58 inches. *Proler/ Oeggerli.* $4,500-5,000.

Ladew Topiary Gardens.

121

Marble figural fountain, early 20th century, rose-colored leaf mottled font surmounted by a figure of a child caressing a swan, with a winged horse. *Ladew Topiary Gardens.*

Victorian lead fountain of a boy playing the bagpipes. *Ladew Topiary Gardens.* Similar fountains have sold at auction for $3,000-5,000.

Italian, antique hand-carved vicenza stone fountain in the form of a boy holding a stylized dolphin, mouth is drilled for water. 24 inches. *Proler/Oeggerli.* $1,200-1,500.

Detail. *Ladew Topiary Gardens.*

Close-up of marble fountain.
Ladew Topiary Gardens

Very elaborate Italian hand-carved vicenza stone two-tiered center fountain. The two scalloped bowls are decorated with four lion head waterspouts raised on a base with four winged horses and surmounted by a cherub finial. 10 feet. *Proler/Oeggerli.* $35,000-38,000.

Stone figural fountain with two cherubs on a tree trunk: one holds conch shell. *Ladew Topiary Gardens.*

A clover shaped pool with lead fountain. *Ladew Topiary Gardens.*

19th century lead fountain. *Ladew Topiary Gardens.*

Ladew Topiary Gardens.

Antique hand-carved Italian vicenza stone two-tiered fountain pedestal with swags and flowers and a pineapple finial. 103 inches. *Proler/Oeggerli.* $30,000-33,000.

Antique Italian hand-carved vicenza stone semi-circular wall fountain bowl with gadrooning. 28 inches. *Proler/Oeggerli.* $1,750-2,000.

125

Italian hand-carved white Carrara marble center fountain, the lower bowl stands on a pedestal trimmed with acanthus leaves, three draped putti hold up the lower bowl, which is surmounted by a cherub fighting with a dolphin. 76 inches. *Proler/Oeggerli.* $33,000-36,000.

Small garden fountain with a lead satyr. Made in England, based on a 19th century original. Pedestal: early 20th century, Italian terra cotta. *Larry Keller.* $500-800.

Detail of above photo.

Late 19th century painted cast iron aquarium center fountain by J. W. Fiske, with paneled sides enclosing a central foliate cast waterspout. The base is a set of encircling cranes. *Ladew Topiary Gardens.* Similar ones have sold at auction for $3,000-5,000.

The Garden Antiquary.

Fountain by J. W. Fiske, zinc, cast iron basin, American, late 19th century. *The Garden Antiquary*. $14,000.

Detail. *The Garden Antiquary*.

Victorian two-tiered cast iron fountain.
Hobensack and Keller.

Modern three-tiered vicenza stone
center fountain. *Proler/Oeggerli.*
$17,000.

Proler/Oeggerli.

Antique, hand-carved vicenza stone two-tiered fountain with three cherubs on a carved base without surround. 91 inches. *Proler/Oeggerli.* $32,000.

A three-tiered painted cast iron center fountain. American, early 20th century. *Hobensack and Keller.* Similar fountains have sold at auction for $8,000-12,000.

A copy of *Young Child with Turtles,* by Estelle Parsons Barretto. Willowbrook Farms, Catasauqua, Pennsylvania.

Late 19th century painted cast iron Victorian garden fountain of two children holding an umbrella.

Cast iron three-tiered central fountain, attributed to J.W. Fiske, American, late 19th century. Central baluster has stylized leaves and fans with three tiers edged with a scalloped border, painted black. *Ladew Topiary Gardens*.

Modern, Italian granite fountain. *Proler/Oeggerli*. $3,000-3,500.

19th century French bronze fountain. *Proler/Oeggerli*. $13,000-15,500.

Villa Reale, Italy

At the end of the day nothing is more soothing than the sound of water in the garden.

Monika Dornan.

Chapter 8
Amphora, Jars, Planters, Urns, Troughs, Vases

Common materials: marble, cast stone, vicenza stone, terra cotta, concrete, cast iron, wood

The desire to display plants and flowers is universal among gardeners. One of the most common garden ornaments are planting containers. Earliest known planters were made from terra cotta. The Greeks and Romans designed elaborate carved urns and pots. Rural gardeners have used everything including discarded feeding troughs.

Urns, overflowing with flowers or as sculptural focal points in a garden, are usually displayed on pedestals.

Proler/Oeggerli.

Villa Reale.

Similar terra cotta pots have sold for $800-1,200. These are at the Hotel Splendido, Portofino, Italy.

Below:
19th century American lead urn with ram head handles. *Hobensack and Keller.* $1,000-1,200.

Villa Reale.

Stoneware planter, probably English. *Proler/Oeggerli.* $3,500.

Villa Reale.

135

18th century terra cotta urn. Villa Reale.

Troughs, limestone, English, late 19th century. Price varies with size. *The Garden Antiquary*. $500 and up.

French terra cotta jar, circa 150 years old. *Proler/ Oeggerli.* $1,600 each.

French terra cotta jar, circa 150 years old. *Proler/Oeggerli.* $1,600 each.

Antique Italian yellow glazed terra cotta olive oil storage jars from Calabria or Sicily. 46 inches high. *Proler/Oeggerli.* $1,800 each.

Two large antique jars or amphora from Turkey, circa 150 years old. 44 inches. *Proler/Oeggerli.* $2,700 each.

Antique terra cotta storage jar from Anatolia, circa 300 years old. 48 inches. *Proler/Oeggerli.* $4,200.

139

Italian, vicenza stone urns with flower decorations on the rim. *Proler/Oeggerli.* $6,500 a pair.

Treetrunk planter, circa 1850, cast iron. This is an unique cast iron American-made planter. Its base shows twisted tree roots. The base is a tree trunk and the bowl has branches. This piece was made by the Miller Foundry in Providence, Rhode Island, as a special twig pattern. *Larry Keller.* $12,000-15,000.

Antique Italian, vicenza stone urn. *Proler/Oeggerli.* $6,000 a pair.

Opposite page, bottom left: Close-up detail.

J.W. Fiske was an important American manufacturer of lead urns and statuary.

One of a pair of planters, limestone, late 19th century, American. *The Garden Antiquary*. $6,500 for the pair.

19th century two handled, cast iron American urn. *The Garden Antiquary*. Similar ones have sold at auction for $3,000-5,000.

Late 19th to early 20th century cast iron urn, signed J.W. Fiske. *The Garden Antiquary*.

The Garden Antiquary.

Double handled urn. William Adams
(1880-1890). *The Garden Antiquary.*
$4,500-6,500.

Hobensack and Keller.

Hobensack and Keller.

19th century Italian vicenza stone planter. *Proler/Oeggerli.* $5,700-6,500.

Italian vicenza stone urn on a pedestal. The urn rises on lotus leaves. *Proler/Oeggerli.* $8,000-8,800.

144

Hand-carved antique Italian vicenza stone single urn on a round base. *Proler/Oeggerli.* $6,500-6,800.

Antique 19th century, Italian, hand-carved, round stone planter with lion heads. 16 inches. *Proler/Oeggerli.* $6,700-7,000.

Antique, hand-carved, vicenza stone planter with foliage decoration, egg and dart trim, resting on lotus leaves with an octagonal base. 30 inches. *Proler/Oeggerli.* $8,000-9,500.

Early 20th century hand-carved melon-shaped vicenza stone campana form on 19th century carved stone pedestal. 41 inches. *Proler/Oeggerli.* $1,500-2,000.

Antique hand-carved vicenza stone urn with gadrooned bowl decorated with egg and dart motif and elaborate scrolled handles. 32 inches. *Proler/Oeggerli.* $5,200-6,000.

Two common urn shapes are the tasse form, a shape that resembles a cup, and the campana form that resembles a bell. Some urns have memorable lids.

Antique melon-shaped campana form urn. One of a pair of Italian hand-carved vicenza stone campana form urns with a gadrooned body on a square base and a egg and dart design on the rim. 27 inches. *Proler/Oeggerli.* $6,000-6,500.

One of a pair of 19th century, melon-shaped urns with a simple rim and a gadrooned body. *Proler/Oeggerli.* $6,500-7,500 a pair.

19th century hand-carved vicenza stone urns. *Proler/Oeggerli.* $6,500 a pair.

Italian, two handled, white carrara marble urn with a fruit and flower swag. *Proler/Oeggerli.* $6,000-6,500.

Single urn, cast iron, American, 19th century. *The Garden Antiquary.* $600-800.

One of a pair of urns on plinths, cast iron, American, late 19th century. *The Garden Antiquary*. $5,500-6,000 a pair.

Antique hand-carved vicenza stone urn carved with ribbon tied fruit and foliage swags with semi-gadrooned bowls on square bases. 28 inches. *Proler/Oeggerli*. $6,200-6,500.

The Garden Antiquary.

Carved vicenza stone planter with four lion heads. *Proler/Oeggerli.* $5,000-6,000.

French 19th century glazed terra cotta Andes planters. *Proler/ Oeggerli.* $1,900-2,200 each.

Hobensack and Keller.

Green glazed terra cotta vases, Southern France. *Proler/Oeggerli.* $1,850-2,000.

The Garden Antiquary.

One of a pair of 18th century-styled lead jardinieres. *Ladew Topiary Gardens*.

Late 19th century, Victorian wood and cast iron three-tiered plant stand. *Ladew Topiary Gardens*.

Italian vicenza stone planter. *Proler/Oeggerli.* $5,700.

Early 19th century Italian hand-carved vicenza stone trough. The rim is carved with rope design, the front panels are carved with columns and two crests, the sides with roses. 54 inches. *Proler/Oeggerli.* $17,500-20,000.

Chapter 9
Wellheads

Common materials: marble, cast stone, vicenza stone, concrete, lead, cast iron, wrought iron

It has been many years since wells had a functional purpose in most gardens, but their appeal has not diminished. Classically-designed elaborate stone wellheads, with ornate cast iron overthrows, can range in price from $6,000 to $20,000.

Cast iron overthrow. *Meadowbloom Gardens.*

19th century Italian, vicenza stone wellhead with grape decorations and a wrought iron overthrow. *Proler/Oeggerli.* $15,000-17,000.

Antique Italian vicenza stone octagonal wellhead complete with octagonal base and wrought iron work. 38 inches. *Proler/Oeggerli.* $13,700-15,000.

Antique Italian vicenza stone round wellhead decorated with four crests complete with a round base and wrought iron work. 34 inches. *Proler/Oeggerli.* $18,000-20,000.

Antique Italian hand-carved vicenza stone octagonal wellhead, the sides carved with birds and stylized foliage complete with octagonal base and scrolling wrought iron overthrow. 34 inches. *Proler/Oeggerli.* $15,700-17,000.

Antique Italian vicenza stone square wellhead in
Renaissance style, hand-carved sides in high relief with
two crests and two vases, a square plinth base and
scrolled with wrought iron overthrow. 25 inches. *Proler/
Oeggerli.* $13,500-15,000.

Antique Italian vicenza stone wellhead in Renaissance style
hand-carved in high relief with stylized flowers, corners
boldly carved with acanthus leaves, the top has a rope twist
border, a square plinth and scrolling wrought iron overthrow. 30 inches. *Proler/Oeggerli.* $22,000-25,000.

Antique Italian vicenza stone wellhead, rim has a rope twist
border, corners boldly carved with acanthus leaves, a square
plinth and scrolling wrought iron overthrow. 30 inches.
Proler/Oeggerli. $22,000-25,000.

157

19th century Italian vicenza stone wellhead, with acanthus leaves in corners, wrought iron overthrow. *Proler/Oeggerli.* $17,000-19,000.

Above and left:
Two sides of an 18th century hand-carved vicenza stone square wellhead, the tapered sides carved with curved arches and alternating carved crests and roses. 33 inches high. *Proler/Oeggerli.* $20,000-23,500.

18th century Italian white Verona marble wellhead complete with columns, pediment and square plinth base. *Proler/Oeggerli.* $35,000-37,000.

Mabel and John Ringling Museum, Sarasota, Florida.

Meadowbloom Gardens.

Monika Dornan.

Chapter 10
Gazebos, Staddle Stones, Gates

Common materials: marble, cast iron, wood

Gazebos

Gazebos and pavillions became popular in the late nineteenth century when outdoor living became more informal. Antique styled gazebos can range in price from as high as $15,000 to $20,000.

Italian stone gazebo, with wrought iron dome. 108 inches. *Proler/Oeggerli.* $24,500-25,000.

Antique Italian hand-carved vicenza stone gazebo, with wrought iron dome. 156 inches. *Proler/Oeggerli.* $25,000-27,000.

Staddle Stones

Most staddle stones are carved from English Cotswold limestone and were used to support barns and elevate the floors so that rodents could not eat the harvest. Almost every barn in England had at least one staddle stone in each corner.

The Garden Antiquary.

The Garden Antiquary.

The Garden Antiquary.

161

The Garden Antiquary.

The Garden Antiquary.

Staddle stones, 18th century Cotswold limestone with circular domes. 30 inches. *Proler/Oeggerli.* $1,200-1,400 each.

Staddle stone, English, hand-carved, circa 19th century. Value is based on the size, shape, and amount of moss and patina on the stone. It is unusual to find pointed tops. *Hobensack and Keller.* $900-2,000.

Gates

Gates, of course, originally had a very important function—that of keeping marauders, both man and beast, away. Later, they had a more decorative purpose that of adding architectural design. Through the centuries they have become important statements of authority, and are frequently ornamented with family and royal crests. Today gates control access to a property, define a space, and are becoming a highly decorative architectual element. Since the late nineteenth century cast iron makers have created gates that are wonderously complex and decorative works of art. One of the most creative and inventive American iron gate makers was Samuel Yellin who worked in Philadelphia in the early twentieth century.

Victorian wrought iron gate. *Ladew Topiary Gardens*. Cast iron gates have sold at auctions for $8,000-12,000.

Left:
Reading Public Museum, Reading, Pennsylvania.

Meadowbloom Gardens.

Ladew Topiary Gardens.

19th century Italian wrought iron double gate. 9 feet. *Proler/Oeggerli.* $23,000-25,000.

Ladew Topiary Gardens.

Ladew Topiary Gardens.

Ladew Topiary Gardens.

Ladew Topiary Gardens.

Left:
Rustic twig cast iron gate pier, mid 19th century, American. *Hobensack and Keller.* $375-800.

Right:
Swan gate. *Ladew Topiary Gardens.*

167

PART THREE—GARDEN FURNITURE
Chapter 11
Chairs, Garden Seats, Benches, Tables

Common materials: marble, cast stone, vicenza stone, cast iron, wrought iron, bent steel, aluminum, wicker, wood

Chairs and garden seating have always been an important part of garden design. Since the days of Jefferson, American ingenuity has created some of the most unique and practical designs for outdoor lounging. Although the Europeans preferred stone, marble, and later cast iron seating, Americans were more pragmatic. In the eighteenth and early nineteenth centuries, it was common practice to bring indoor chairs outside for lawn entertainments. One of the most common "outdoor" chairs was the simple utilitarian Windsor-styled chair. Rocking chairs were also a popular American invention and early rockers were simply that—chairs attached to bent rockers.

It was the Industrial Revolution and mass manufacture of cast iron designs that changed American garden seating. By the mid-1830s practical -minded Americans were buying cast iron settees, arm chairs, side chairs, and tables. One of the most interesting innovations was a cast iron tree surround bench, a semi-circular bench made to fit around a tree trunk.

Cast iron appealed to Americans' practicality. It was cheap, easy to maintain, weatherproof, and durable. On the other hand, elaborate Italianate marble benches and tables appealed to those who preferred the more grandiose schemes of formal entertainments.

One of the first and most popular cast iron manufacturers was the English company Coalbrookdale, located in Shropshire. By the 1840s, the company had its first patent for a new style of cast iron furniture in a variety of color finishes—green, brown, and bronze. The company also offered their products in a variety of natural botanical images such as a grapevine, berry, laurel, oak leaves, horse chestnuts, lily of the valley, nasturtium, and fern patterns.

One of the earliest American companies to make cast iron seating was J.L. Mott Company, which got its first patent in 1847 for a revolving cast iron armchair. Another important cast iron manufacturer was the New York firm of J.W. Fiske and Company.

The Victorians loved ornate cast iron designs. And soon chairs, benches, and tables had elaborate patterned legs, often copying the acanthus leaf, which is a design often found on classical marble fountain and urn basins. Seats either had wooden slats or ornate cast iron patterning.

The Victorians embraced nature from afar and developed a fondness for artificial contrivance. The rustic look was popular, but not the rustic life. Chairs with twig legs, arm rests, and back rests were popular. Chairs resembling tree trunks also became a popular stylistic trend.

Another popular garden style of the day was the Gothic style, which resembled the ornate and highly patterned look of Victorian interiors. Influenced by Gothic architecture, the Gothic look favored pointed arches, fleur-de-lis, and a lot of complex piercing and open fretwork. Furniture also had animal claws and feet as arm rests and leg supports.

Another form of the Gothic style in cast iron garden seats was the curtain style garden bench, which resembled an old-fashioned window curtain or a throne chair. Today good cast iron can range in price from as little as a few hundred dollars, depending on condition, age, and pattern, to upwards of several thousand dollars.

Another modern stylistic development was wire-work and bent steel chairs. The French were leaders in creating elegant outdoor seating. As a society they enjoyed sitting outside in cafes, and their outdoor cafe chairs led the way in inventive designs. Two of their most popular cafe chairs were wire-work chairs and the spring-back, balloon-back chairs. Wire-work chairs had delicate ornate scrolls for legs and backs. The French also created another breezy informal look with a spring-back chair called the Sunburst or Balloon chair. These chairs have become very popular in home gardens. Today there are still many modern reproductions.

By the late 1920s, the modernists stamped their influence on the outdoors with a new series of seats made out of tubular iron rods and bent steel.

Richard Schultz's 1966 Leisure Collection for Knoll Furniture revolutionalized outdoor garden furniture design. These streamlined sculpural designs embody the ultimate in form, function, and easy to maintain care. Lightweight, durable, and impervious to weather, this line, which is now part of the Museum of Modern Art collection, is considered the most well-regarded collections of outdoor garden furniture!

Schultz's newest designs, the Topiary line and the Confetti line (not pictured), were made from sheet aluminum with cut-out designs, and can be viewed as a 1990s extension of Victorian cast-iron furniture. Schultz's chairs range in price from $500 to $2,500.

Today prices for garden furniture range from $400 to upwards of $1,200. It is difficult to differentiate between the nineteenth century originals and some very good twentieth century reproductions.

Today many wealthy homeowners still prefer the formal look of the Italian marble antiques. Antique Italian marble pieces can sell from $8,000 to upwards of $20,000.

Chairs and garden seating have always been an important part of a gardening design. Since the age of Thomas Jefferson, American ingenuity has created unique designs for outdoor lounging. Windsor chairs were used outdoors as well as indoors. Rocking chairs were found on covered porches and pavilions. Garden chairs were designed for easy maintenance, with open fretwork, simple legs, and graceful seats.

Ladew Topiary Gardens.

Meadowbloom Gardens.

Victorian gardeners liked romanticized versions of nature in their gardens. This is an unusual grouping of early 1920s stone furniture, cast to look like trees and flowers. These four chairs and a center table, circa 1910, loosely represent the four seasons. Each chair back has flowers, cornucopia, berries, leaves, and birds. The table base is cast as a tree trunk wrapped with leaves. *Ladew Topiary Gardens.*

1950s cast iron chair and table. Fogelhaus, Center Valley, Pennsylvania. $500-800.

1950s cast iron chair with animal. *Hobensack and Keller*. $150-200. Dog is cast stone: $155.

Late 19th century cast iron chair with grape design. $300-500.

Coalbrookdale painted cast iron garden furniture is usually priced to sell at $1,500-2,000. Since this furniture was so durable, and was just left outside on porches, patios, and lawns, many pieces are available today.

Above left:
Modern reproduction.

Left:
1950s table.

Meadowbloom Gardens.

Dog's head cast iron chair. This is very unique. Only two are known to exist. The other is in New York's Metropolitan Museum of Art. *Larry Keller.*

Detail.

Cast iron grape design table, 19th century, Victorian style. Probably originally had a slate or marble top. *Larry Keller*.

Below:
Victorian cast iron center table and swivel arm chair, late 19th century, American. The table has a leaf border. The armchair has a pierced back of scrolls and flowers and cabriole legs. *Ladew Topiary Gardens*.

20th century cast iron tree surround with a design of berry leaves on grapevine-formed legs. *Ladew Topiary Gardens*.

20th century, circa 1950s, American, white painted wire chairs. *Ladew Topiary Gardens*. Pieces like this usually sell for $800-1,200.

Meadowbloom Gardens.

20th century American white painted scroll back wire garden seat with matching chair with balloon back seats. Note the back of the bench has a circular scroll pattern as well. *Ladew Topiary Gardens*.

174

A modern reproduction. *Hobensack and Keller.*

American Sunburst chair, circa 1950s. *Proler/ Oeggerli.* $300-350.

1920's designed chair. Lanark Manor. $1,000-1,500.

Mesh Rocker, handmade wire mesh, American, early to mid 20th century. *Hobensack and Keller.* $175-250.

Early 20th century chairs. *Anthony Garden Boutique*. $200 each.

Modern reproduction.

Modern twig chair.

Meadowbloom Gardens.

20th century Adirondack chair. $500-800.

Right:
Meadowbloom Gardens.

Early L.L. Bean fishing
chairs. Lanark Manor.

The following photos are by Richard Schultz.

Richard Schultz chaise lounges, 1966 collection. Lanark Manor. $2,000-3,000.

Richard Schultz 1966 Leisure collection.

Richard Schultz Topiary collection.

1930s Warren McArthur
chairs. Lanark Manor.
$2,000-5,000.

184

Benches

Keukenhof Gardens, Holland.

Cast iron furniture came in many designs—grapes and berries, Gothic, twig or rustic, fern, lily of the valley, nasturtium, water plants, or the curtain patterns.

Ladew Topiary Gardens.

Cast iron furniture set, American, 19th century. *The Garden Antiquary.* $2,000-2,500.

Late 19th century cast iron love seat, American. It is very unusual to find a bench this small. *Hobensack and Keller.*

Detail.

Curtain style, cast iron bench, 19th century, American, signed Island City, Brooklyn. *Hobensack and Keller.* $1,400-1,750.

19th century cast iron bench with an unusual scroll and crest design.

20th century American, cast iron bench with an American fern pattern showing interlacing ferns. *Ladew Topiary Gardens*.

Late 19th century cast iron painted twig bench in the rustic style. *Ladew Topiary Gardens*. Similar pieces have sold for $800-2,000.

20th century American painted cast iron garden seat. The back has a cluster of berried grapevines on a circular seat with berry formed legs. *Ladew Topiary Gardens*.

20th century American painted cast iron garden bench with a floral design seat that has a circular pierced design. *Ladew Topiary Gardens*.

Cast iron French botanical garden bench. Late 19th century reproduction. *Hobensack and Keller*.
$2,000-2,350.

Stone garden bench with egg and dart pattern and scrolled supports. *Ladew Topiary Gardens.*

Three stone garden benches with griffin supports. *Ladew Topiary Gardens.*

189

Cast stone garden bench. *Ladew Topiary Gardens*.

Ladew Topiary Gardens.

Ladew Topiary Gardens.

Modern rustic style twig garden bench.

Lytens style oak seat with an arched back and scrolled arms. Similar benches have sold at auction for $2,500-4,000.

191

Modern wooden garden benches.
Ladew Topiary Gardens.

1920s American designed wire garden bench. *Meadowbloom Gardens*.

Cast stone garden bench with scrolled leg supports. *Ladew Topiary Gardens*.

Dallas Arboretum, Dallas, Texas.

193

19th century Italian vicenza stone garden bench based on an antique Florentine design. *Proler/Oeggerli.* $13,000-15,000.

19th century Italian, vicenza stone garden bench with a lion mask backplate and stylized scrolled leg supports. *Proler/Oeggerli.* $10,500-12,500.

Old Italian hand-carved vicenza stone curved bench with backplate, lion paw bases, egg and dart border on the seat. *Proler/Oeggerli.* $23,000-25,000.

194

Antique Italian vicenza stone, curved stone bench, 13 feet. *Proler/ Oeggerli.* $25,000-30,000.

Antique Roman Renaissance style Gallo Istria marble lion seat, circa 1900, 32 inches high. *Proler/Oeggerli.* $20,000-23,000.

Urs Oeggerli in one of his favorite classic Italian seats.

18th century, Italian, hand-carved Rosso Verona marble bench with Renaissance Roman lion supports and grape motif detail, 85 inches. *Proler/Oeggerli.* $30,000-37,000.

Center:
Antique Italian Renaissance Rosso Verona marble oval bench raised on two lion bases, 200 years old, 57 inches. *Proler/Oeggerli.* $15,000-18,700.

The Garden Antiquary.

Note the lion supports.
Old Westbury Gardens.

Old Westbury
Gardens.

Glazed terra cotta bench, American, early 20th century. *The Garden Antiquary*. $7,800-8,000.

The Garden Antiquary.

Marble bench. *The Garden Antiquary.* $4,500-4,700.

20th century reproduction cast stone bench with sphinx supports. *Hobensack and Keller.* $200.

20th century reproduction cast stone bench with lion supports. *Hobensack and Keller.* $300.

Late 19th century Italian Verona marble garden table, 30 inches. *Proler/ Oeggerli.* $19,500.

199

19th century table supports, 31 inches. *Proler/Oeggerli.* $4,500 a pair.

Monika Donnan.

PART FOUR—TWENTIETH CENTURY GARDEN KITSCH
Chapter 12
Jockeys, Folk Art, Kissing Dutch, Gazing Globes, Concrete Animals, and Flamingoes

Common materials: cast stone, concrete, lead, cast iron, wrought iron, wood, plastic

Today it seems as if every garden has at least one garden ornament—be it art or kitsch. Gazing globes have been popular in gardens since Victorian times. Wishing wells have also been popular garden accessories, as have cast iron fountain sculptures of children, often with turtles, dolphins, or umbrellas, and cast iron and concrete flamingoes, first popular in the 1920s. In the 1930s, Tramp art, intricate wooden carvings made by unemployed "tramps" or hobos during the Depression, became popular. Concrete farm animals, cast iron jockeys, and composite donkeys and burros have been popular since the 1940s and 1950s. Plastic flamingoes became popular in the 1970s. Today one of the newest trends is "back views of ladies." Another has been an increase in seasonal decorations on homes, lawns, and in gardens. Who hasn't been amazed by the proliferation of Halloween extravaganzas with RIP (Rest in Peace) tombstones and witches and ghosts fluttering in the wind? Or Irish leprechauns? Or Easter bunnies popping out of bushes? And even old sailors at the gateposts of a home?

Is it art or kitsch? Is it too much?

We'll let you decide.

Pricing garden folk art is difficult. Prices are determined by the market. Vintage garden ornaments sell from $50 up to $500. Collectors buying habits stem from the nostalgic to the fanciful, the whimsical and the outrageous.

Wouldn't a saucy, kissing Dutch couple in your garden make you smile, too?

Outhouses have been called privies, necessaries, and other such euphemisms. During the colonial period many wealthy landowners surrounded their outhouses with columns, porticos, and even enclosed them in Greek temples. This is a very primitive 20th century rural outbuilding in Pennsylvania. The Beck Garden.

Left:
A 20th century
painted cast iron
jockey. $500-800.

1940s vintage cast iron jockey. *Hobensack and Keller.* $800-1,000.

A 20th century Mexican terra cotta mask. The Pondhouse. $100-150.

Modern sculptures. *Meadowbloom Gardens.*

"Bending Ladies" are one of the latest fads to pique the attention of modern gardeners. $25-40.

An Irish leprechaun.

A modern cast stone "beastie." *Hobensack and Keller*. $200.

1950s, American, painted concrete lawn ornament of a cardinal. Concrete animals became popular lawn and garden ornaments during the late 1940s and 1950s. The most popular forms were farm animals, birds, and donkeys. $50-75.

Terra cotta Mexican folk art. The Pondhouse. $100-200.

Modern "beasties," cast stone quartz with hand made copper collars with chain links. *Hobensack and Keller*.

Since the 1920s when pink flamingoes were introduced to Florida, flamingoes have become popular collectibles. 1920s cast iron and cast stone flamingoes sell for $200-350. Plastic flamingoes can cost as little as $5.00.

Tramp art crows, wood, 1980s. The Pondhouse. $75-100.

Florida folk art "wiggler." $100-125.

For over two hundred years, birdhouses have been made to resemble a variety of buildings, such as barns, country stores, and folk art fantasies. Prices range from $50-200.

Donkeys have been popular lawn orna-ments since the 1950s.

A modern interpretation of an armillary. *Sam Kenworthy, Meadowbloom Gardens.*

A composition stone cowboy. The Wagon Wheel Motel, Jackson, Wyoming.

Sarasota Jungle Gardens, Sarasota, Florida.

A modern fish waterspout. *Meadowbloom Gardens*.

1950s, painted wire figural garden chairs showing the influence of Matisse and Picasso. *Ladew Topiary Gardens*.

1950s, painted wire figural garden chairs showing the influence of Matisse and Picasso. *Ladew Topiary Gardens*.

Nothing is more inviting than an old-fashioned porch swing to enjoy a garden. *Barbara Strawser, Schaefferstown, Pennsylvania*.

Cast iron designs first became popular during the Victorian era. Americans created wonderfully colorful fantasies such as this piece of cast iron gating. $50.

Gazing globes have been popular garden ornaments since the turn of the century. Fogelhaus, Center Valley, Pennsylvania.

Toad Hall, Allentown, Pennsylvania.

Stone and steel
mushrooms. The
Pondhouse.

Ladew Topiary Gardens.

Left:
Seasonal garden accents.

Ladew Topiary Gardens.

Weathervanes come in many styles. This barnwood airplane was made by folk artist David Stuckey. The Pondhouse. $500.

"Time spent fishing don't count," David Stuckey. The Pondhouse. $400.

"The Gardener," 20th century painted bronze, American, Seward Johnson. *Philip and Muriel Berman Collection.*

The end of the day.

A GARDENER'S PRAYER
Thank You God for Sun and Showers
Thank You for Each Lovely Flower
Thank You for Each Stately Tree
Through All These, You Speak to Me

Sarasota Jungle Gardens, Sarasota, Florida.

223

Monika Doman.

Resources

Anthony Garden Boutique Ltd.
134 East 70th Street
New York, New York 10021
212-737-3303

Lexington Gardens
1011 Lexington Avenue
New York, New York 10021
212-861-4390

Moshe Bronstein
The Garden Antiquary
724 Fifth Avenue
New York, New York 10019
212-757-3008

Charleston Gardens
Lewes, England

Hobensack and Keller
P.O. Box 96
57 Bridge Street
New Hope, Pennsylvania 18938
215-862-2406

Ladew Topiary Gardens
3535 Jarretsville Pike
Monkton, Maryland 21111
410-557-95706

Meadowbloom
Snowdenville, Pennsylvania 19475
610-495-5187

Proler/Oeggerli
2611 Worthington Street
Dallas, Texas 75204-1015
214-871-2233

Richard Schultz Design
Palm, Pennsylvania 18070-0096
215-679-2222

We also are indebted to Sotheby's and Christie's auction houses. Their sales catalogs have been an invaluable source of information.

Christie's East
219 East 67th Street
New York, New York 10021
212-606-0400

Sotheby's
1334 York Avenue
New York, New York 10021
212-606-7000

Bibliography

Baker, Martha. *Garden Ornaments.* New York: Clarkson Potter Publishers, 1999.
Hill, May Brawley. *Furnishing the Old-fashioned Garden.* New York: Harry N. Abrams, Inc., 1998.
Israel, Barbara. *Antique Garden Ornament: Two Centuries of American Taste.* New York: Harry Abrams, Inc., 1999.

Russell, Vivian. *Edith Wharton's Italian Gardens.* New York: Bulfinch Press Book, Little, Brown and Company, 1997.
Smith, Linda Joan. *Garden Ornaments.* New York: Smith & Hawken, Workman Publishing, 1997.
Williams, Bunny. *On Garden Style.* New York: Simon Schuster Editions, 1998.